Original title:
Iris Ideals

Copyright © 2025 Creative Arts Management OÜ
All rights reserved.

Author: Arabella Whitmore
ISBN HARDBACK: 978-1-80566-694-3
ISBN PAPERBACK: 978-1-80566-979-1

The Poetry of Growth

In a garden of dreams, I plant my socks,
Hoping they'll sprout into talking rocks.
They giggle and tumble, they dance on the ground,
A chorus of chuckles, a whimsical sound.

I water my plants with lemonade streams,
They grow extra arms and play hopscotch with beams.
The daisies wear hats, the tulips all prance,
A party of petals in a flowery dance.

The carrots wear glasses, the radishes sing,
They boast of the laughter that springtime can bring.
While beans tell tall tales of reaching the sky,
And lettuce just giggles, too shy to comply.

So join in the fun, let your garden come play,
With laughter and joy in the light of the day.
For growth is a journey, a quirky parade,
Where each little sprout is a joke that we've made.

Hidden Harmonies

In a field where daisies dance,
Bees wear hats, they prance and prance.
Butterflies with shades of blue,
Debate on who is the best to woo.

The grass claims it's the star today,
While clouds just drift as if to say,
This world of silly, bright delight,
Keeps laughter ringing, morn till night.

Nature's Reflections

A squirrel dons a tiny vest,
While flowers giggle in their quest.
The pond reflects a fish with flair,
Practicing dives like he's a player.

Trees gossip softly in the breeze,
Exchanging secrets with such ease.
They laugh as leaves begin to sway,
In nature's chatty cabaret.

Vibrations of Color

Crayons gather for a show,
They argue who can steal the glow.
Red claims it's quite the fiery rage,
While blue just waves from center stage.

Green insists on leafy tunes,
To sway in sync with fluffy dunes.
As rainbows form a jolly band,
It's color chaos, oh so grand!

Nurtured Notions

In gardens where the thoughts grow tall,
Ideas bloom and often sprawl.
A gnome who guards a playful thought,
Whispers whimsy, never caught.

Sprouts of laughter in each patch,
Tangle with dreams, a vivid match.
Hence, in this land of giggles bright,
Nurtured notions take to flight.

The Spectrum of Hope

In a garden of giggles, colors collide,
A rainbow of dreams, let's take a ride.
With every hue, a joke to share,
Laughter blooms brightly, floating in air.

Banana peels slip on our blue delight,
While the green grass tickles, oh what a sight!
Crimson clowns dance with a silly tune,
As the sun winks down, bright as a balloon.

Reflections in a Purple Lake

A purple pond sits, glassy and sly,
With fish wearing hats, oh my, oh my!
They splash silly stories, ripples entreat,
As frogs croak in rhythm, oh what a beat!

Lily pads giggle, a comedic flair,
In this wacky kingdom without a care.
Tadpoles recite lines like stars in a show,
While turtles play cards, just taking it slow.

Echoes of a Colorful Mind

In the mind's kaleidoscope, thoughts have a play,
A slapstick parade in a zany display.
With shades of green giggles and violet grins,
Each chuckle's a treasure, where comedy spins.

Yellow ducks quack wise with a punchline or two,
While orange cats tumble, causing hullabaloo.
Pink clouds bring laughter, floating sky-high,
In this colorful realm, no one can be shy.

Visions Beneath the Bloom

Under petals of laughter, bright secrets reside,
Bumblebees buzz with mischief as their guide.
Jokes bloom like daisies, playful and sweet,
Oops! A flower sneezed – pollens in retreat!

With daffodil hats and a sunflower tie,
Garden gnomes chuckle, oh me, oh my!
Petal with a wink, punctuates a jest,
In this lively patch, who's really the best?

Luminous Thoughts in Petal Form

Dancing dreams in hues of blue,
Petals whisper secrets, just a few.
A butterfly with socks on tight,
Giggles sparkle, oh what a sight!

Sunshine with a twist of zest,
Flower hats, we'll wear the best.
Twirling in the garden's cheer,
Silly faces, bring us near!

Dances with the Lavender Breeze

Lavender twirls in the sunny glare,
Socks mismatched, no one would care.
Winking clouds with cheeks so round,
They giggle softly, joyous sound!

Chasing dreams on a breezy day,
Floppy hats in bright array.
With lavender laughs that never cease,
We'll dance along, a quirky lease!

The Heart's Chromatic Journey

A heart that races with colors bright,
Dance shoes on, oh what a sight!
Pinks and greens in playful fight,
Chasing rainbows, pure delight!

Skipping stones on laughter's stream,
With every hop, we find a dream.
Throw confetti into the air,
Savor the quirks that love can share!

Fragments of a Celestial Canvas

Stars paint giggles in the night,
Brushes made of pure delight.
Clouds parade in sparkly views,
Waves of laughter in pastel hues!

Twinkling tales on warm spring eves,
Jigs and jumbles, playful heaves.
With starlight's wink and moonlight's cheer,
We sketch our joy, year after year!

The Poetry of Color

In a world where hues collide,
I found a blue that winked with pride.
Red danced around like a clown,
While green just sulked, wearing a crown.

Yellow laughed, spilled all its cheer,
Orange blushed, holding a beer.
Paintbrushes fight in a colorful mess,
Who knew this palette could cause such stress?

Every shade has its own tale,
Some are smooth, while others flail.
Mix them up, and chaos reigns,
With splashes of joy and colorful pains.

Ethereal Fragrances

The scents of life swirl in my nose,
A whiff of fun in every rose.
Lilac giggles, lavender snores,
While citrus zips in through the doors.

Chocolates tease like flirty fiends,
Minty fresh, oh how it gleans!
Pineapple tickles, sends me reeling,
With every breath, there's the funny feeling.

A bouquet of laughter fills the air,
But watch out for the smelly pair.
Garlic and onion take the stage,
Turning this party into a fragrant cage.

Canvas of the Heart

My heart's a canvas, painted wide,
With splatters of joy, I can't hide.
A dash of love, a stroke of glee,
And a real big blob of mystery.

Silly doodles dance on the page,
While serious thoughts sometimes engage.
Crayons argue, who's the best shade?
And the paint spills have all been laid.

Every heart has its own design,
With awkward lines that intertwine.
Mix in some giggles, a stroke of fate,
Watch as my colored heart radiates.

Silhouettes of Ambition

In shadows cast by dreams so bright,
Figures leap, ready for flight.
A jester jumps, aiming for fame,
While the scholar's lost in a bookish game.

Dancing to tunes of success ahead,
But tripping on thoughts that've been widespread.
Confidence swells like a balloon,
Yet pops with a laugh—oh, what a tune!

Each silhouette tells a funny tale,
Of hopes and dreams that sometimes fail.
Ambitions twirl like a waltzing sprite,
With shadows laughing in the moonlight.

Colorful Reveries

In a world where socks don't match,
Clowns juggle eggs without a scratch.
Rainbows sprout from every beat,
As jellybeans dance on candy street.

Balloons wear hats, they float with flair,
A cat wears trousers, oh what a pair!
Lollipops whip up a sugary cheer,
And giggles echo, loud and clear.

Blossoming Dreams

A pancake flip that feels just right,
With syrup rivers flowing bright.
Cacti wear shades in the sunny glow,
While broccoli sings in a high falsetto.

Surreal cupcakes frolic in the sun,
As broccoli debates, who's having fun?
The toaster pops out bread with style,
While squirrels groove, all the while.

Visions in Bloom

A monkey drives a tiny car,
Sipping tea under a giant star.
Marshmallows bounce in a playful race,
While clouds put on a pillowcase.

Socks take tango lessons with shoes,
Jellyfish wear party hats of blues.
The sun wears glasses, looking bemused,
As daisies cheer, all enthused.

Unfolding Potential

A penguin slides down a rainbow slide,
With ice cream dreams and unicorn pride.
Glitter storms rain from cotton clouds,
While laughter gathers up the crowds.

Teapots whistle, brewing delight,
As cookies dance into the night.
Octopus plays chess with a mime,
In a topsy-turvy world, oh how sublime!

Lush Landscapes of Emotion

In gardens where the colors clash,
The daisies wear their polka dot sash.
A tulip whispers to a shy rose,
"You've got stamen? I suppose!"

Chasing butterflies in a wild race,
The sunflowers giggle, a silly face.
"Who knew we'd be a flower show?"
Dandelions waltz, stealing the glow.

Laughter blooms between the greens,
As mushrooms do the dance of beans.
Peonies puff up with great pride,
While violets blush and try to hide.

The breeze plays tag, round and round,
A silly dance without a sound.
In this lush land, joy takes flight,
As petals party deep into the night.

The Secret Language of Petals

In the world where flowers converse,
Roses brag, while daisies rehearse.
"I can twist!" a petunia shouts,
"But I can flip!" blurted out spouts.

Orchids roll their eyes with glee,
As lilies try to sip their tea.
"Your perfume? What a silly prank!"
While violets blush, avoiding rank.

Tulips gossip, then shout and cheer,
"Wait, did you hear? The bees are here!"
Petals flutter, buttons undone,
A flower brawl, but all in fun!

In the garden of tales, where chaos reigns,
Blooming amigos, breaking their chains.
With every hue, a laugh takes flight,
In secret tongues, they giggle all night.

Harmonious Exuberance

The blooms all hum a cheerful tune,
While bees and bugs dance beneath the moon.
Dandelions twirl, free and bold,
While bumblebees barter for tales untold.

Sunflowers sway with exaggerated grace,
While grasshoppers hop to keep up the pace.
A marigold shouts, "I want the lead!"
But a quiet bluebell just takes heed.

"Watch me!" cries a brave little sprout,
As he leaps and tumbles without a doubt.
While others laugh on the sunny green,
The snickers rise like a joyous sheen.

In this quirky world, the flowers blend,
Their joyous giggles will never end.
With colors bright and spirits high,
They dance and play, reaching for the sky.

Vibrant Shadows

In a patch where colors collide,
A zany peony jumps, giddy with pride.
Frolicking past, a bold marigold,
Says to a carnation, "Are you too old?"

As petals peek out from leafy tents,
Deciding who's where, with no pretense.
A witch hazel cackles, old and spry,
While a shy fern gives a grunt and sigh.

"Oh, look! It's a tulip conga line!"
Shouts a daffodil, quite a sly design.
Colors twinkle like stars in the night,
While shadows dance, a beautiful sight.

Laughter echoes beneath the trees,
As blossoms chuckle in the breeze.
In this garden of vibrant hues,
Even the shadows have joyous views.

Whispers of the Violet Dawn

As morning breaks with laughter bright,
The flowers giggle in soft light.
Waking bees with buzzing cheer,
They dance around without a fear.

A dandelion wearing a frown,
Complains about a bee in town.
'You're stealing nectar, can't you see?'
To which the bee just sips with glee.

The sky, a canvas painted blue,
With clouds that play peekaboo.
A butterfly trips on a breeze,
Catching laughter among the leaves.

In the garden, joy's the norm,
Where whimsy and laughter take form.
With every laugh, the flowers sway,
Inviting fun to fill the day.

The Palette of Dreams

In dreams we splash with colors bold,
Drawing stories yet untold.
A painter's brush, a cheeky grin,
Making magic as we begin.

Canvases of giggles and sighs,
With rainbow faces and silly eyes.
A splash of purple, a swirl of gold,
Creates a tale that never gets old.

They say that wishes come with flight,
Like a kite that dances, oh so bright.
With every tug and every twist,
The palette spills, it's hard to resist.

Embracing dreams without a care,
Sipping magic from the air.
Each stroke a chuckle, each hue a cheer,
In this wild art, the fun draws near!

The Language of Flowers

In a garden of giggles, blooms unite,
Twirling petals in the soft sunlight.
Roses whisper jokes to daffodils,
While tulips dance, oh what a thrill!

Peonies tell tales of bees in a buzz,
Sunflowers laugh, as if they were fuzz.
Daisies toss petals, oh such delight,
Sprinkling laughter in pure bloom's light.

Violets chuckle in shades of blue,
As pansies tease with a playful view.
Each blossom blooms with a quirky grin,
Floral humor is where fun begins.

In this flowered haven, laughter grows,
Where every stem and leaf knows how it goes.
Nature's comedy, at every turn,
Telling tales for us to learn.

Blossoms of Daring

In the land of petals, brave blooms stand,
Daring to reach for sunshine so grand.
Fearless lilacs stretch beyond the norm,
While zinnias giggle, defying the storm.

Raggedy roses wear thorns as hats,
Cacti crack jokes, oh what fun for bats!
Each flower boasts of its daring feat,
Flirting with winds, they dance to the beat.

Poppies pop up, not one bit shy,
Challenging gardens to give it a try.
With every bloom, a riotous flair,
Quirky nature's grand, wild affair.

In this floral circus, laughter rings,
Each daring petal has fun in their flings.
Join the blossoms, take heed of their ways,
In a world of flowers, laughter stays.

Mystical Murmurs

In twilight gardens where secrets play,
Whispering blooms have much to say.
Lilies chuckle, weaving spells so fine,
While nightshade giggles over a glass of wine.

Petals murmur tales of ancient lore,
With hidden puns no one can ignore.
Sweet begonias hint at mischief near,
With winks and nods, they spread the cheer.

Orchids wink, such mysterious sights,
While cosmos twirl in their starry flights.
Each blossom holds a joke, a theme,
In the night, they play, a vibrant dream.

Mystical murmurs weave through the air,
Where laughter lingers with each petal's care.
Join the midnight bloom, let secrets be,
In this floral realm, there's fun to see.

Spectrum of Possibilities

In a kaleidoscope of hues so bright,
Petals gather for a comedy night.
Crimson and gold share the limelight fair,
While emerald leaves wiggle without a care.

Lavender laughs at the mint's sweet tease,
As daisies create a whimsical breeze.
Flirting with colors, each tone sings loud,
Reveling in the joy of a blooming crowd.

Clever chrysanthemums plan a prank,
While lilacs throw sprinkles from the tank.
In this vivid spectrum, fun lights the scene,
Each flower's dream is a humorous glean.

Join the show, where colors collide,
In this dance of blooms, we must confide.
With laughter ringing in the petals' spree,
The spectrum of fun is wild and free.

The Aesthetic of Hope

In a garden where dreams collide,
The daisies dance, the roses hide.
A bee in shades of neon bright,
Claims he's a knight, ready to fight.

With pots of gold and hooks of fate,
The gnomes sit laughing, oh what a state!
They sip on tea brewed with a twist,
Every sip, a giggle, not to be missed.

Beneath the sun, the shadows play,
The sunflowers wave in a derpy sway.
A ladybug with polka-dot pride,
Takes a selfie for the world wide.

Resonance of the Bloom

Petunias gossip, oh my dear,
Chattering tales of garden fear.
A squirrel in shades, striking a pose,
Claims he's the ruler, everyone knows.

The tulips giggle, swing and sway,
Mocking the clouds in a fluffy fray.
A rogue dandelion starts a rave,
While the wind is the DJ, bold and brave.

The roses blush, not just for show,
For a bumbling bee stole their glow.
They hold a meeting, a secret affair,
With snacks of nectar, oh how to fare!

Harmonies of the Garden

In the patchwork quilt of earth and sky,
The violets croon, a lullaby.
Worms tap dance, not missing a beat,
While ants form conga lines down the street.

A radish jokes about its roots,
With leafy friends, they share their truths.
The carrots flex their leafy green,
In a veggie contest, that's the scene!

With whispers sweet, the petals cheer,
As butterflies flutter, oh so near.
In this concert of colors so bright,
Each bloom holds laughter, pure delight.

Whispers through the Leaves

The oak tree chuckles, wise and old,
Sharing the tales of the brave and bold.
A chipmunk squeaks, "Did you hear that?
The breeze just made my favorite hat!"

With rustling secrets, the willow sways,
While crickets beat a tune for days.
Mice in tuxedos throw a ball,
While fireflies twinkle, catching it all.

Leaves gossip softly in afternoon's glow,
As the sun dips low with a playful bow.
In this woodland soirée, life's a jest,
Laughter in petals, nature's best.

Whispers in the Amber Air.

In a garden filled with sweet despair,
A squirrel ventured, unaware of a dare.
He danced on a branch, oh so spry,
While the cat below began to sigh.

Breezes carried laughter up high,
As butterflies giggled, passing by.
They painted the sky with colors bold,
While ridiculous jokes in whispers unfold.

A ladybug wore a tiny hat,
Claiming he's quicker than any old cat.
He boasted he'd run a race today,
But tripped on a leaf and lost his way.

In the amber air, mischief galore,
Chasing shadows, they always explore.
For in this realm of playful delight,
Nothing is wrong, and all feels right.

Petals of Perception

Petals drift down with a sassy flair,
They giggle and twirl through the sun-kissed air.
A bumblebee sports the latest style,
Dancing through blooms with a clumsy smile.

Insects debate on who loves the most,
The daffodil argues like a boastful ghost.
Roses roll eyes at the fray of the day,
While tulips gossip in a snooty display.

The daisies form a committee so grand,
To write the strict rules of flowerland.
But when they bloom, those rules go astray,
As petals argue all through the play.

In the garden of hues where wild dreams sprout,
It's clear that laughter is what it's about.
With petals of humor and blooms full of cheer,
We'll dance through the moment, year after year.

Garden of Dreams

In a garden where wishes are planted with glee,
The sunflowers chatter like they own the marquee.
They share the juiciest tales of the day,
While the moon peeks through, getting ready to play.

Dandelions dream of quite silly things,
Like wearing tiaras made out of springs.
And little worms tap dance on the ground,
To the rhythm of leaves where laughter is found.

The lizards wear shoes of shimmering fun,
While shade trees gossip, "Can you believe he won?"
The blooms join in, a colorful crowd,
Sprouting their quirks, oh so joyously loud.

In this paradise where oddities reign,
Each petal's a punchline, never mundane.
With each whimsy bloomed in the warmth of the sun,
The garden abounds with joy never done.

Spectrum of Thoughts

Thoughts flutter like kites in the bright azure,
Whirling with nonsense, of that I'm sure.
The green ones say bananas have wings,
While the pinks strut around, oh, what silly things.

The blues claim they've found a fountain of youth,
But it turned out to be just a talking tooth.
The yellows, convinced they're the funniest shade,
Tried telling a joke, but all they displayed.

In a swirl of colors, laughter does bloom,
With thoughts on the edge of whimsical doom.
Bartering puns like a grand bazaar,
Trading in chuckles beneath a bright star.

As the sun dips down, the hues intertwine,
Each giggle a note in a fanciful line.
For in this spectrum where absurdities play,
Every spark of laughter paves a new way.

Sprouting Thoughts

In the garden, thoughts take flight,
A lettuce hat worn just so right.
Carrots giggle from underground,
With vegetable jokes that astound!

Blob of mud, my new best friend,
He promises to stick till the end.
A flower sneezes, and pollen flies,
I chase them down with big, wide eyes!

Bees wear glasses, what a sight!
They sip sweet nectar day and night.
With tiny scooters, they zip around,
Spreading laughter in buzzing sound!

With each sprout comes a silly tale,
Of radishes wearing rubber veils.
In this patch, where laughter's fed,
Even broccoli cracks a joke instead.

Serenity in Bloom

Daisies dance in the gentle breeze,
Telling secrets to clumsy bees.
A tulip trips, falls on its face,
But gets up, its pride in place!

Petunias gossip, their colors bright,
About a sunflower's late-night flight.
They claim he's stashed snacks in his seeds,
And sways to the beat of garden deeds!

In the shade, a lazy bumblebee,
Plays checkers with a ladybug, you see.
They laugh at the ants who pass them by,
Waving flags made of leaves, oh my!

The roses blush, so full of charm,
As they prickle each other, causing harm.
In this garden where joy's in the air,
Even weeds wear bows, oh how they dare!

Beneath the Blossoms

Underneath where petals sway,
Bunnies frolic, bright and gay.
They play hide and seek with bees,
Who gently buzz among the trees!

A dandelion goes on a spree,
Wearing a crown, brave as can be.
He's the king of leafy jesters,
Making jokes about wild wrestlers!

A tulip tells of dreams in flight,
While laughing at a cloud so white.
"I'll catch you, fluff!" the petal shouts,
As dew drops dance and swirl about.

Beneath the blossoms, fun's in bloom,
Growing laughter, dispelling gloom.
With every giggle, colors pop,
In this cheery garden, never a stop!

The Dance of Light and Shadow

In the garden, light and shade,
Waltz together, a fluffy parade.
A shadow cracks a joke at dawn,
And giggles as the sun moves on.

Laughter echoes from sky to ground,
Chasing cheeky raindrops around.
While daisies burst in colors rare,
A mischievous breeze yanks at their hair!

The sunbeams play tag, oh what a sight,
Tickling petals, day turns to night.
Fireflies join with sparkling cheer,
Dancing in rhythm, drawing near!

In this garden, joy takes flight,
As shadows giggle at the fading light.
With moonlit whispers and soft glow,
The dance goes on, and laughter flows!

Luminescence of Ideas

Bright thoughts dance in my head,
Like fireflies on a Friday night.
When genius strikes, it's often said,
That socks and sandals feel just right.

Ideas twirl like spaghetti strands,
They jump and wiggle, make me grin.
In crazy realms where humor stands,
I find the quirkiest wins begin.

Jellybeans and wacky schemes,
Mixing colors in a stew.
Laughter flows like ice cream dreams,
In the world of funny and new.

Balloons rise high, the visions soar,
My brain's a circus, loud and bright.
Who knew that thoughts could win the war?
As crazy as a fruitcake fight!

Ephemeral Expressions

A doodle here, a sketchy line,
Whimsical moments, lost in grace.
Tiny fables, oh how they shine,
Like marshmallows in outer space.

Jokes scribbled on the backs of hands,
Ephemeral, they fade away.
Like pop-up books in rusty bands,
They crack me up, come out to play.

Laughter hangs, a gentle breeze,
Like petals tossed from silly trees.
Each smile blooms with great ease,
In randomness, we find our keys.

A giggle here, a snicker there,
These fleeting thoughts, they spark delight.
In the end, who needs despair?
We'll laugh our way into the night!

Roots of Aspiration

Digging deep in playful soil,
My oddball dreams take root and sprout.
With every crack and twist and toil,
I find new things to laugh about.

Potatoes dress in silly hats,
And carrots sing in happy tunes.
With radish dreams and charm like cats,
My garden's full of goofy boons.

Each sprout is weird but oh so grand,
A patchwork of my wildest hopes.
In wobbly chairs, we make our stand,
Fulfilling dreams with twists and ropes.

Lettuce laughs when wind goes wild,
Planting joy with every seed.
Come join the party, sweet and mild,
Where fun and laughter often lead!

Nature's Palette

Colors splatter on the scene,
With purple cows and pinkish trees.
In this wacky art machine,
Every brush stroke brings us glee.

The sun wears shades, a silly hat,
While clouds giggle, soft and round.
Nature whispers, "How about that?,"
As butterflies break into sound.

Grass tickles with its vibrant hue,
As paints collide and joy ignites.
In every splurge, we start anew,
Creating laughter, day and night.

So let's embrace this wild display,
Where colors blend in playful ways.
With laughter lighting up the day,
Nature's art is where joy stays!

The Light of Perspective

A pigeon asked the sun so bright,
"Why do you shine? What's your delight?"
The sun just grinned and winked a ray,
"To light up birds who eat gourmet!"

A cat once thought it could sing high,
But only croaked like a frog nearby.
The frog just laughed and said, "Not true!"
"Your meows will make a great stew!"

The clouds like pillows float on by,
While squirrels debate how to fly.
"With acorns as wings, we'll take a chance,"
"Or we will make a mess of this dance!"

Let's pull back the curtain and just sit,
Life's absurdity is truly a hit.
Laughter dances in the air so sweet,
With every bizarre thing on the street.

Petal-Soft Realities

A daisy dreamed of being a queen,
Wearing a crown of vibrant green.
Its petals swayed in regal pose,
While ants giggled at its fancy clothes.

In the garden, a snail raced fast,
Claiming it's the champion at last.
But a tortoise rolled his eyes and sighed,
"Slow and steady wins, or so they've lied!"

The bees buzzed on about their beeswax,
While butterflies threw shade with their tracks.
"You call that flying? What a tease!"
"At least we don't need a GPS, please!"

In the midst of this floral debate,
A sunflower grinned, "Isn't it great?"
To ponder life in shades so bright,
Funny how things buzz in daylight!

Pondering in Petals

A lily wondered how it would bloom,
While sitting in a garden room.
"Do I need a party? Or a fan?"
"Maybe a song? Or a disco plan?"

A rose piped up with prickly cheer,
"Let's make it wild; I'll bring the beer!"
So they danced, twirled, and spilled some dew,
With petals flying, oh what a view!"

A windchime sighed, "What's all the fuss?"
"A flower party? Who'd dare to miss?"
The grass giggled and swayed on cue,
"This garden's alive with dreams anew!"

So they pondered what the petals say,
Laughter echoing, come join the play!
In every color, in every laugh,
Life's nonsense blooms, a vivid craft.

Gentle Currents of Thought

A stream flowed by with a giggle and splash,
Wit as sharp as a pebble's clash.
"It's thinking time! What's the next prank?"
While frogs plotted a clever bank.

A willow tree whispered, "Don't drop my shade,"
As the bumblebees came, unafraid.
"Here's some pollen, our sweet design,"
"It's not just honey; it's a funny line!"

Clouds rolled in for a surprise show,
With jokes that only the raindrops know.
"It's pitter-patter party time!"
As laughter echoed, not a single rhyme!

So here underneath the leafy glen,
We find the laughter time and again.
With gentle currents, thoughts flow free,
In nature's whimsy, there's joy, you'll see!

Flourishing Horizons

In gardens where the daisies dance,
A gopher's grin, a funny prance.
They think they're kings, the critters boast,
But grass stains mark their little hosts.

With sunhats on, the ants parade,
A conga line where snacks are laid.
They form a band with pots and pans,
Beating rhythms with tiny hands.

The clouds up high make silly shapes,
Like rubber ducks and flying grapes.
We dream of pies and silly things,
While wind beneath our laughter sings.

As colors burst in vibrant glee,
The world is light, and so are we.
Life's simple joys, we can't ignore,
Let's cartwheel 'til we hit the floor.

Mosaics of Mindfulness

With whims and wiggles, ducks align,
In orderly chaos, we intertwine.
A mix of colors as bright as dreams,
A jigsaw puzzle of giggling beams.

We scoot on scooters, laughter loud,
As clouds above form a fluffy crowd.
The squirrels giggle, they dance with flair,
While cacti wear their funniest hair.

A teacup spun on a turtle's back,
With rainbow sprinkles, it's quite the snack.
Whirling thoughts like colors play,
In this strange realm, we laugh away.

Mindful moments in a silly form,
Where bubbles pop and chickens swarm.
Finding joy in little quirks,
As humor hugs us, smiles and smirks.

The Blooming Essence

A daffodil with disco moves,
Bobs its head as the green grass grooves.
The bees create a buzzing beat,
They've got the funk, they can't be beat!

In the vegetable patch, quite a sight,
Carrots juggle, trying with all their might.
Tomatoes roll in a rhythm fine,
As lettuce cheers with a square dance line.

Petunias wear their brightest hats,
While rhubarb cracks up at silly chats.
Dandelions puff like little suns,
They float away with goofy runs.

With every petal, every flick,
Nature's humor plays a trick.
Life's a garden, wild and fine,
In every laugh, the sun will shine.

Flourishing Fantasies

In this land where dreams collide,
A dragon wears a sparkling slide.
He crackles jokes and lights the night,
With candy clouds, it's pure delight.

A unicorn with roller skates,
Zooms around, while friendship waits.
In silly hats, the critters cheer,
They trade their giggles without fear.

Sprinkles rain down from cotton trees,
Lemonade streams flow with the breeze.
Marshmallow mountains stand so tall,
Where laughter echoes like a call.

Life's a carnival, come join the ride,
With every twist, our worries slide.
So let us dance beneath the sky,
In fruitful fun, we'll soar and fly.

A Dance with Hues

In a field of colors bright,
Dancing flowers take to flight.
They twirl and spin, a merry throng,
Who knew that plants could groove along?

With tippy toes, they sway so high,
Winking at clouds in the azure sky.
Butterflies giggle, sipping nectar sweet,
While bees join in with the funky beat.

Petals pop like corn in a pan,
What a wild, cheerful flower clan!
They throw a party, no need for a fuss,
"Let's have a blast!" they gleefully discuss.

As dusk drapes a shimmer over the scene,
The flowers whirl, what a sight to glean!
In the garden's glow, they don't feel shy,
"Let's bloom and burst, oh my!

Blooming Aspirations

Once a bud with dreams so grand,
It wished to travel to some far-off land.
It practiced its dance, a charming delight,
With hopes to perform 'neath the moonlight.

But winds said, "No, just stay in place!"
In the garden, find your space.
Still, it plotted, with wink and nod,
"Tomorrow's my day; I'll give it a prod."

Along came a snail with a twinkling eye,
"Your dreams are so big; don't let them pass by!"
With humor and cheer, they set off together,
"We'll navigate life, no matter the weather!"

And so they laughed, the bud and snail,
Setting up shop on a concrete trail.
For even a bloom in the dirt can see,
That laughter can sprout, wild and free!

Reflections in Lavender

Oh lavender fields, so calm and grand,
With whispers of fragrance all over the land.
They gossip of dreams, both big and small,
As the bees buzz in for their nightly ball.

"Who wore what?" they titter and tease,
While the sun dips low and the night brings ease.
With a wink and a nod, the moon takes a seat,
Listening close to their lavender beat.

"Tomorrow I'll shine!" declares a bold sprout,
As it stretches its petals and shakes out a doubt.
"I might even pose for a magazine!"
The lavenders laugh, "Oh, you little queen!"

As stars twinkle soft, with a wink and a sway,
They dream of more stories to share every day.
In the still of the night, all is carefree,
A lavender world, wild as can be.

Tapestry of the Soul

In a patchwork quilt of colors bright,
Every thread tells a tale of delight.
With patterns of laughter and patches of cheer,
Each stitch holds a secret, so precious, so dear.

A dandelion fair had a whisk of a dream,
To float to the stars, or so it would seem.
"But wait!" cried a violet with petals askew,
"We've not done the tango, how can we break through?"

So they spooled out a dance of frisky old glee,
While the daisies applauded, "Oh, look at they!"
With every twist and every turn,
They taught the wind a thing or two to learn.

At twilight, they joined in a swirling parade,
Celebrating friendship, never to fade.
In a tapestry woven with giggles and fun,
Under the moon, together they spun.

Dreamscape of Petals

In a garden full of noodle blooms,
Squirrels dance to smelly tunes,
Bees wear hats, they're quite bizarre,
Chasing dreams of a jelly jar.

Petals giggle in the breeze,
Ticklish leaves fall from the trees,
Butterflies play hopscotch up high,
While turtles plot how to touch the sky.

Daffodils tell secrets like spies,
Roses throw pies, oh what a surprise!
Sunflowers gossip with the sun,
About how trees just wanna run.

In this land where silliness reigns,
Every flower has its own refrains,
Join the fun in this petal spree,
Where laughter blooms eternally.

Kaleidoscope of Whispers

Whispers travel on the breeze,
Tickling ears like summer tease,
Chirping frogs wear fancy suits,
While crickets play the funny flutes.

Clouds are gossiping, so it seems,
About the squirrels stealing dreams,
Snails wear shades, they think they're cool,
In this odd little garden school.

Dandelions blow wishes, oh dear,
But wind has a laugh, can't stop the cheer,
They trip on roots, fall down in style,
Create new paths that make us smile.

Colors swirl like candy rain,
In this world of fun and gain,
Nature winks with every breeze,
Let's dance along with rustling leaves.

The Allure of Nature

Nature's charm, so full of glee,
Invites us in for tea and spree,
Ants parade in clever rows,
While blooming laughter freely flows.

The sun wears shades but burns bright,
Moon snores softly, quite the sight,
Trees tickle clouds, what a delight,
Hummingbirds zoom by, taking flight.

Pinecones crack jokes, trees shake their limbs,
Rabbits throw parties, but no one swims,
Every creature has a role,
In this show of nature's soul.

Join the fun, don't be a bore,
Dance through blooms, let your heart soar,
For in this realm of sweet allure,
Nature sings—of that we're sure.

Growing Beyond Boundaries

Plants in pajamas, what a sight,
Stretching out under stars so bright,
Bouncing beans jump up and say,
'Who needs rules? Let's play today!'

Vines wrap around old fence posts,
Waving hands, they cheer the most,
Roses giggle, forget to bloom,
While daisies sing away the gloom.

Gnomes in gardens break-dance, who knew?
Puppies dig holes for a magic view,
Every border just a guideline,
In this land where joy is divine.

So let's grow wild, twist and twirl,
In this colorful, crazy whirl,
Nature giggles, and so shall we,
For boundaries fade, we roam free.

The Vibrant Palette of Dreams

In a land where colors play,
Brushes dance in bright array.
Green thinks it's the star of the show,
While pink just giggles, 'Hello, hello!'

Orange sneaks in for some fun,
Squirting lemon juice on the run.
Blue pretends to take a nap,
But wakes with a splash—what a trap!

Each hue is plotting schemes and plans,
Painting rainbows with their hands.
But wait! What's that? A splash of gray,
"Not today!" the colors shout in play.

So let them battle, yell, and scheme,
In this wild and wacky color dream.
With laughter echoes, they'll explore,
Creating shades worth looking for!

Shades of Reflection

In the mirror, colors clash,
Red thinks green is a bit brash.
Yellow giggles, twirls around,
Leaving blue to pout and frown.

Reflecting on a joyful scene,
The shades debate who's the queen.
"Lavender forth, take your throne!"
But little gray just moans, 'Alone!'

See, every hue has its own flair,
Except for fuchsia, who just stares.
"Why am I here, so bold yet shy?"
A splash of pink just sighs, "Oh my!"

So in this glass of endless hues,
Each color picks its favorite shoes.
With mismatched socks and crazy paint,
They prance around without restraint!

In the Company of Blossoms

Beneath the sun, a flower crew,
Gathered round for a color brew.
Daisy wears her polka dots,
While tulip snickers, 'Who needs spots?'

Peony sings a silly tune,
While lilacs dance, swoon and swoon.
Sunflower says, "I'm just too cool,"
And picked up a round hat, a school!

Roses have a secret game,
With thorns, they stake their claim to fame.
But violets laugh, "It's all okay!"
As petals swirl in bright bouquet.

So every bloom with quirks is found,
In blooming laughter, joy abounds.
With petals rustling, all agree,
A garden's where they all feel free!

The Harmony of Hues

In a cafe where colors meet,
Orange serves up tangerine treat.
Red orders a cherry delight,
While blue brings muffins that take flight.

"Not too sweet!" Green can't stand,
Sipping tea, making a stand.
Purple whispers, "Add some flair!"
With sprinkles flying everywhere!

The manager—who happens to be gray,
Rolls his eyes as he sweeps away.
"Stop the fun, you silly crew,
You'll scare the customers, it's true!"

But laughter spills from every cup,
In a world where colors mix it up.
For harmony, they make a toast,
And sip their drinks, laughing the most!

Whispers of the Violet

In the garden of dreams, where colors collide,
A purple potato oddly decided to hide.
It whispered to daisies, "Oh, life is so sweet!"
They chuckled and danced, tapping their feet.

A squirrel in a top hat did jive with a bee,
While pondering which shade of mauve was the key.
The breeze took a sigh, made petals all twirl,
And butterflies cried, 'This is better than pearl!'

A bluebird recited a poem on a tree,
About the blend of wild fig with brie.
The roses turned red, then burst into giggles,
While honeybees buzzed in vibrant wiggles.

So if life's a patchwork of hues and of cheer,
Remember the violet that whispered so dear.
For laughter and color in gardens abound,
In the zany parade where joy can be found!

Enchanted Blooms

In a patch of bright lilacs, the toads all convene,
To discuss the latest in lily aesthetics unseen.
They've formed a firm union, the Lilac Lit Guild,
To read froggy romances until all are thrilled.

The daisies wore boots with sparkles and flair,
They danced like they just didn't have a care.
A tulip in shades of neon and glow,
Attempted to start a wild flower show!

A gnome with a flute led a conga line,
While mischievous pixies threw blossoms of wine.
"Let's toast to the petals!" the lilies would cheer,
As butterflies swirled, drawing laughter and beer.

So next time you wander through gardens so bright,
Pay heed to the blooms and their magical flight.
For laughter abounds where the flowers reside,
In enchanted corners, let joy be your guide!

Echoes of Color

In a realm of marigolds, bright as the sun,
A cactus once asked, "Is it okay to run?"
The orchids were clueless, the daisies perplexed,
As the rose shrugged and said, "Well, get off the flex!"

A daffodil dressed in a tuxedo of gold,
Told tales of the blooms that gathered and rolled.
The poppies fell over, laughing so hard,
While tulips played charades in the family yard.

A rainbow kicked back, sipping tea with a breeze,
Giggling at clouds that were pulling the sleaze.
"Why focus on gloom when we can paint the blue?"
Asked a zany sunflower, "Join me, will you?"

For in this loud garden, where colors do sing,
There's joy in the chaos, like frogs playing king.
Let's spread the wild laughter, like seeds in the air,
In echoes of color, all worries lay bare!

Veil of Beauty

In a land full of tulips, where pranks never cease,
A daisy declared that she'd reign as the niece.
With petals of velvet and laughter so grand,
She dazzled the critters, the whole garden band.

A bumblebee monarch wore sashes and crowns,
While gathering pollen with whimsical frowns.
"Be careful!" cried roses, all pink and all sweet,
"That regal bee's hungry and loves royal treats!"

The violets snickered, with heads held so high,
Making tales of the day when a shrub learned to fly.
"Imagine the sight!" squealed a sprightly young bud,
As the petals erupted in a giggling flood.

So wander through gardens with laughter and grace,
Where petals of beauty light up every space.
For laughter's the flower that blooms ever bright,
Behind every veil, there's a comical sight!

The Language of Lavender

In gardens bright with lavender's sway,
Bees buzz around, in a dance of play.
Whispers of color, a fragrant release,
Each bloom a giggle, nature's own tease.

Petals in purple, a sight so sweet,
They gossip with daisies, share tales of feet.
A lavender wink, a playful surprise,
With colors so bold, they brighten the skies.

In pots and in fields, they giggle aloud,
Tickling the toes of the wandering crowd.
With sun hats and smiles, they sway in the breeze,
Lavender's laughter is sure to please.

So join in this frolic, let colors ignite,
Dance with the blooms, celebrate the light!
With lavender's tone, a joy to unfold,
Each laugh, each hue, a story retold.

Beneath the Veil of Hues

Under the arches of vivid delight,
Colors conspire, a comical sight.
Blues make a joke to the greens as they joke,
Oranges chuckle, while purples just poke.

In secret they meet, all shades in a whirl,
Brushes and paints begin to unfurl.
A canvas on which they can all take a stand,
In laughter and mischief, they mingle so grand.

Splatters of fun, a riot on white,
Each shade a prankster, it's pure comic light.
They lighten the mood with a flick and a swirl,
The riot of colors, a blooming world.

So join in this joy, beneath vivid skies,
Let laughter and colors be your allies!
Be bold, be silly, let hues have their say,
In this wacky world, come laugh and play!

When Blooms Speak Truth

Petals converse in a secretive way,
With stories of sun and the games they play.
Lilies jest with roses, an amusing debate,
Who blooms the best? It's a floral fate!

In the still of the night, they whisper so loud,
Confessions of love make them feel proud.
Daisies nod knowingly, in their white frocks,
While tulips just giggle, hiding behind clocks.

Chasing the bees, they plot and they scheme,
For nectar and sunshine, a shared golden dream.
The petals unite, in a colorful fight,
With blooms that declare, "We've got it just right!"

So listen closely, when blossoms break free,
Their laughter so sweet, it's pure jubilee!
In gardens or fields, let friendship take root,
With blooms that are silly, we savor the fruit.

Silhouettes of Serenity

In twilight's embrace, the flowers take flight,
Shadowy figures in the dimming light.
They dance in the night, a comical sight,
With petals like cloaks, they twirl with delight.

Beneath the soft glow, they whisper and sway,
Gardens are chuckling, in their own funny way.
Each silhouette grins, with a secret to share,
In the corners of calm, laughter fills the air.

Their whispers float high, like balloons in the breeze,
Tickling the stars, doing as they please.
Joined by the moonlight, they share in the scheme,
For laughter and blooms are a wonderful dream.

So linger awhile, in the glow of the night,
Let flowers invite you, to share in their light.
With whispers and giggles, a soft serenade,
In silhouettes of peace, let harmony wade!

Where Blooming Ideas Take Flight

In a patch of dreams where giggles grow,
Ideas sprout up, all in a row.
One shouts, 'Look! I'm an orange duck!'
The other replies, 'Just my luck!'

A paper flower flutters, bold and bright,
It says, 'Why not take a small flight?'
With a banana peel as our slick slide,
We soar through clouds, taking it in stride.

The daisies dance, the tulips sing,
Claiming boldness is the best of bling.
'Forget the rules!' the sunflowers shout,
As they spin and twirl about.

So grab your hats, let's skip along,
With flowers that insist we can't go wrong.
In the land where jests bloom like carrots,
Every thought is a chortle and all are ferrets!

A Symphony of Color and Thought

A bluebird chirps in a violet haze,
Singing tunes of amusing ways.
With each note, a color appears,
Painting laughter that tickles our ears.

An orange sun winks from the sky,
While daisies gossip as they pass by.
'Is that a bee in a top hat there?'
'Why yes, I heard he's quite the heir!'

Lavender lilies join the fun,
Juggling thoughts under the sun.
The giggles rise like a hot air balloon,
As we float through this colorful afternoon.

So let's unleash our wildest dreams,
In a garden where nothing is as it seems.
With hues and tones that tease the mind,
In this symphony of laughs, let's unwind!

Unraveling the Threads of Whimsy

In a world where socks and flowers blend,
Each petal's a joke; come, let's amend!
A crocus insists it can recite a rhyme,
While roses giggle; it's never a crime.

An unruly vine twists round a tree,
Telling tales of how wild it can be.
'Just yesterday,' said the clever fern,
'I taught a snail how to dance and turn!'

Slip on a polka dot, take a chance,
Join the daffodils in their merry dance.
With threads of laughter woven in air,
We're fabrics of whimsy, without a care.

So gather your dreams, your quirky hats,
In this garden of giggles where silliness chats.
Unravel your thoughts till they burst like balloons,
With cheer as our goal, like cartoon raccoons!

Melodies in the Garden of Colors

In gardens where colors play hide and seek,
Bumblebees buzz in their bowties, so chic.
A chocolate fountain flows, oh what a sight!
With jellybean paths that twinkling ignite!

Roses howl at the bright yellow sun,
'Hey there, buddy! Let's all have fun!'
A marigold whispers with secret delight,
While petunias plan a dramatic flight.

Caterpillars in sunglasses strut with pride,
As the daisies chuckle, no need to hide.
They sing the tunes of colors so loud,
Filling the air, like confetti, unbowed.

So let us gather, both odd and neat,
In this vibrant garden where laughter's a treat.
With melodies blooming from laughter's sweet core,
We'll dance and play, forever wanting more!

Transcendence in Bloom

In a garden where socks dance,
Petunias wearing a cartoon glance,
Dandelions tell secrets of old,
While tulips tiptoe, cheeky and bold.

Bees buzzing jokes, all in good cheer,
Roses giggle — 'What's that noise, dear?'
Crickets perform a nighttime ballet,
While night blooms whisper, 'We're here to play!'

Sunflowers gossip under the sun,
'Look at that daisy, what's he done?'
Violets laugh, 'We're sweet and demure!'
While lilacs claim, 'We smell way more pure!'

At the dusk of this floral delight,
Everything's crazy, but feels just right.
Join this world adorned by whimsy's loom,
In the heart of the garden, no room for gloom.

The Palette of Being

A painter's brush leaps and twirls,
Creating chaos with color swirls.
Geraniums giggle in shades of red,
While daisies poke fun at their bed head.

The poppies whisper, 'Look at my hat!'
'You think that's stylish?', giggles the cat.
"Why wear petals when you can wear lace?"
Said the crazy marigold in pink space.

Butterflies flaunt their mismatched flair,
Flapping around without a care.
The world's a canvas; it's not all prim,
With laughter splashed on every whim.

Jokes unfold in this vibrant zone,
Nature's humor, forever our own.
Color us silly, with joy on display,
In this silly garden of blissful ballet.

Shades of Serenity

In a field where the daisies jest,
Each flower believes it's the best dressed.
Lavender rolls on a soothing breeze,
While pansies chuckle in twinkle of keys.

The lilies sigh, 'We just can't compete!'
Narcissus smirks, 'Aren't I so sweet?'
Ferns fan themselves with leafy delight,
While violets whisper, 'Let's stay up all night!'

Roses argue over who smells divine,
Chatting in colors that somehow align.
Heard a sunflower's tall tale on the way,
It blurted, 'I'm the tallest, what do you say?'

In this realm where blooms dream and play,
Serenity dances in the light of day.
With humor uplifted by nature's own charms,
We find the warmth in these floral arms.

Enigma of the Flora

In the depths of mystery, blooms abound,
Petals debating what's lost and found.
'Who wore it best?' a daffodil spoke,
While hydrangeas giggled, 'That's quite the joke!'

Tulips twirled in a confused trance,
As violets attempted a clumsy dance.
Forget-me-nots thought, 'What's with the fuss?'
But hugged the laughter, all in good trust.

Sunset paints with an artist's flair,
Bright colors blushing, with flair to spare.
Conversations sprinkled with whimsy and lore,
As the delicate petals beg for encore.

In this garden of puzzling delight,
Flora confesses, 'We're silly, alright!'
Beneath the surface, the laughter's profound,
In the enigma where joy can be found.

The Symphony of Blooms

In the garden, a flower plays,
With swagger that brightens the gray.
Bees buzz like a funky band,
While petals dance, oh so grand!

They wear hats made of dew,
And chat about the morning view.
The tulips laugh, the daisies sing,
It's a floral jamboree, a riot of spring!

Caterpillars waltz with a flair,
While grasshoppers giggle without a care.
With each bloom, a joke takes flight,
Colors clash in comic delight!

So come and join this leafy crew,
For laughter blooms bright, as flowers do!
In this garden, every day's a show,
Where giggles and petals simply flow!

Aesthetic Echoes

In a world where colors collide,
A quirky rose took a wild ride.
Wearing shades of purple and green,
She chuckled at the colorful scene.

Daffodils wore their silly hats,
While sunflowers danced like acrobats.
With petals shimmering like disco balls,
They threw a party, inside four walls!

Butterflies giggled, taking turns,
As the marigolds spun and churned.
In this meadow of vibes galore,
Nature's laughter echoed more!

Oh, the wind, it whispered a tune,
As the daisies swayed under the moon.
Join this grove of bright delight,
Where every glance ignites the night!

Celestial Gardens

Up in the sky, the flowers plot,
A field of stars in a cosmic spot.
With comets trailing in petals' sway,
They toast to the night, hip-hip-hooray!

Moonflowers glow with a giggly cheer,
As fireflies join in, bringing light near.
Jupiter winks at the playful blooms,
While Saturn spins in its vibrant plumes.

Even the clouds can't help but laugh,
At blossoms making up a silly staff.
A league of colors, gleaming and bright,
Turning stardust into sheer delight!

So raise a glass in this galactic grove,
Where laughter blossoms and dreams rove.
Among the stars, let joy ignite,
In these gardens of cosmic light!

Embracing the Vibrance

In a cacophony of colors bright,
Zinnias bounce in pure delight.
They wear stripes with spots all around,
Fashion icons of the floral town!

Petunias giggle, swaying free,
Their neon hues, a sight to see.
A bumblebee's a jester, look at him go,
As he jazzes up each bloom, in a show!

Every leaf hops with a silly cheer,
In this garden, there's no trace of fear.
Buds burst open in a riotous fun,
Creating a symphony under the sun!

Join in the dance, don't loiter or wait,
For every petal spins with fate.
In this vibrant land, where colors play,
Laughter blooms wildly, day after day!

www.ingramcontent.com/pod-product-compliance
Lightning Source LLC
Chambersburg PA
CBHW071848160426
43209CB00003B/464